ABC
Mindful Me

Christiane Engel

SCHOLASTIC INC.

What does it mean to be mindful?
Follow us through the alphabet and
you will see—practicing mindfulness
is as simple as A–B–C!

Awareness

Pay attention to your world,
It's full of surprises
Beautiful things in all shapes and sizes!

Breathe

It's a joy to be alive!
Breathe in, breathe out.
That's what it's all about!

Compassion

Spread your love,
Show that you care—
Compassion is for us to share.

Dream

Dream with us,
Let your thoughts fly—
Together we can reach the sky.

Energy

Pay attention to your energy.
Is it high or very low?
Either way, just remember it will always flow.

Feelings

How do you feel?
Angry, happy, sad, or stressed?
These rocks with faces might help you express.

Giving

DONATIONS welcome

Giving is fun!
You've grown out of your clothes?
Maybe someone else would like to have those!

Helpful

Try being helpful.
Do something for free.
It feels amazing—you'll agree!

Inspire

Get inspired by nature!
Find some leaves, a stick, or two—
You'll be surprised at what you can do!

Joy

Joy is all around you!
Find it in the little things,
And feel the happiness it brings.

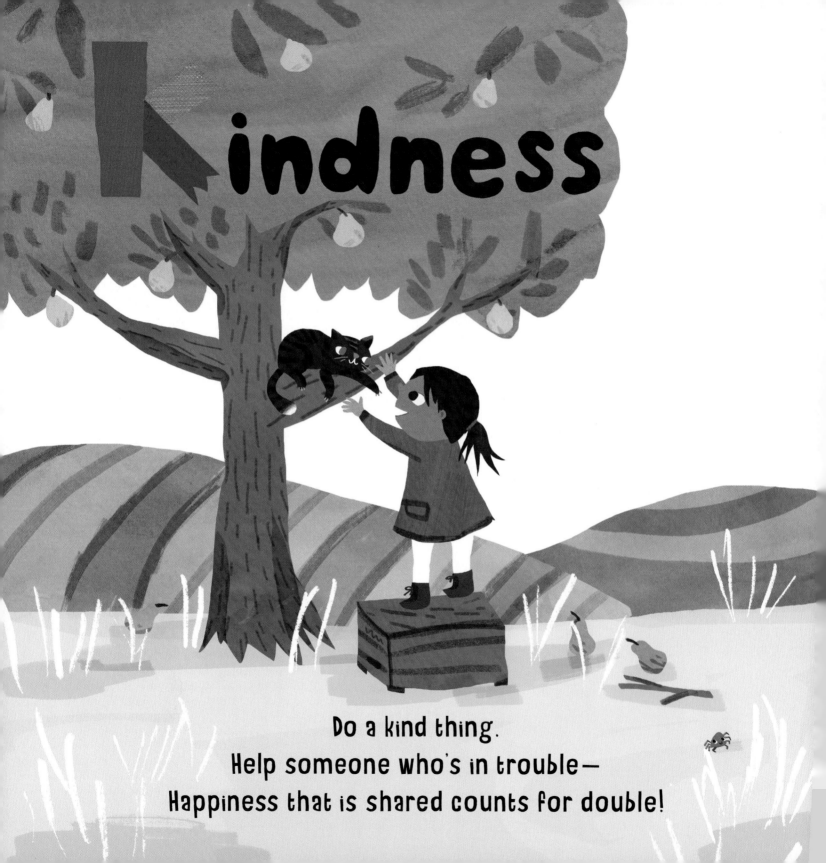

Kindness

Do a kind thing.
Help someone who's in trouble—
Happiness that is shared counts for double!

Love

Love is wonderful.
It brings us together,
And it stays in our hearts forever!

Meditation

Find your inner peace—
Be still, breathe in the fresh air,
Meditation will guide you there!

Namasté

Close your eyes,
Bow to your heart.
Thank you all for taking part!

Outdoors

Let's play outside!
Whatever the weather—
It will surely make you feel a bit better!

Present

Let go of your worries—
Be present in the here and now.
Making a mandala can show you how.

Quiet

Enjoy the silence.
Settle down and take a rest.
In your quiet place, you'll feel blessed.

Relaxation

Move to the music.
Stretch in your own special way.
Make relaxation a part of your day!

Sleep

Go to sleep, arms and hands,
Go to sleep, legs and feet—
May your dreams be fun and sweet.

Thankfulness

What is it you are most thankful for?
Be sure to tell your family and friends:
Being grateful never ends.

Universe

Everyone is part of it!
No matter how big or small—
The universe connects us all.

Vegetables

From a seed into a plant—
Healthy veggies for my tummy.
Thank you, Earth, they are so yummy!

Walk

Go out and take a mindful walk—
Carefully listen, look, and smell.
Amazing things you'll have to tell!

 # marks the spot

There's a special place in nature,
Waiting just for you—
Explore and be curious, and you'll find it, too!

Yoga

Plank like a crocodile,
Stretch like a tiger —
Practice yoga and you'll feel wiser!

Zen

Be one with your body,
Be one with your mind—
Oh, what happiness you will find!

what is
Mindfulness?

Being mindful means paying attention to the present moment, which will help to calm your mind and body so you can find peace and happiness within yourself. Mindfulness can be practiced by taking a walk, breathing, or meditating. By being mindful, you'll be able to better understand your emotions and worries. Awareness of the world around you will also help you to have a positive attitude and be more compassionate.

ISBN 978-1-338-50327-2

12 11 10 9 8 7 6 5 4 3   19 20 21 22 23 24

Printed in the U.S.A.   40

First Scholastic printing, January 2019